MSKOZE / RED SHE IS

Kathryn Dohrmann

Copyright 2025 Kathryn Dohrmann
ISBN: 978-1-957863-57-3

Please comply with copyright laws and do not reproduce, scan, photograph, or distribute this book in any form without permission from the author and/or publisher. (Though we do encourage quoting your favorite lines with proper citation in book reviews or referencing this book, again with proper citation, in academic research.) Parisian Phoenix does not support the use of our intellectual property for the training of artificial training intelligence technologies or systems.

The author, publisher and artists involved with the production of this book appreciate reader support.

Parisian Phoenix Publishing, Easton, Pennsylvania

FOR ED AND ADRIAN

*When I don't know what to do,
I go to the plants.
To learn from the land,
you need to be in the presence of a teacher.*

Robin Wall Kimmerer

TABLE OF CONTENTS

Introduction   1

POEMS:

The Flower   3

Air From Another Life and Time And Place   4

She And *Nanokshi*   7

Mrs. Spoon and Mr. Smith   9

Barefoot   11

Red She Is   13

Mskoze   15

Migwéch   16

NOTES   19

BIBLIOGRAPHY   39

ACKNOWLEDGMENTS   41

ABOUT THE AUTHOR   40

INTRODUCTION

I wanted to find an Indigenous name for *Lobelia cardinalis*. Commonly called Cardinal Flower, this plant is native to much of the Americas. The search for an Indigenous name was not as simple as I'd imagined. It became a journey into ecology, ethnobotany, language, history, and colonization. Down a magic well I went, with a plant as a teacher.

In my search I wished to honor local knowledge. I looked to the Potawatomi nations, for whom this place is home. I like to think that the very oldest trees in my neighborhood once heard the lush sounds of Potawatomi language.

As I searched, poems arose. They varied in form, as if they had minds of their own. There was also energy created in the process of, as Joy Harjo terms it, "knowledge gathering," and it, too, required a voice. This energy resulted in the notes that follow the poems.

I write from the perspective of a non-Indigenous person, and I remain concerned about using words and ideas that do not belong to me. I have chosen, however, to trust my plant guide. This plant comes to me as "She." In the poems, "She" and "Her" always refer to the plant, which I also call, "The Flower."

THE FLOWER

> *...plants are thought of as beings with their own histories, stories, beliefs, and ways of life. Anishinaabe protocols require us to introduce plants just as we would introduce another human being.*
> Wendy Makoons Geniusz

See Her red flares
vibrating in the green
opposites

on a divine color wheel
singular
as the red bird in the cedar

You will meet Her
in deep woods, in places
where ground floats

and mud steals shoes
swamp oaks
and cypress

heavy beyond measure
forest
filigreed with light

AIR FROM ANOTHER LIFE AND TIME AND PLACE

*...the strange blooms they loved
so much set seed in the rich dark
mulch of human desires...*
Jennifer Potter

*...And sometimes in our water dreams,
we pitiful land-dwellers in longing recall,
and singing make spirits ready
to follow; bakobii**
(*Go down into the water.)
Kimberly M. Blaeser

i
A rustic, a *cantadora*, an old woman
will whisper
stories of the Mistaken Zygote —
seed in the wrong soil
embryo in exile
lonely child dreaming of a different family
the swan hatched among ducklings
the swan its own exquisite self —
a strange bloom
called by the wrong name

ii
Early in the 17th century, royal gardener
John Tradescant the Younger
collected The Flower
as he forayed tidewater
Virginia's backways
with his Powhatan wife
Suckahanna
— the name means water —
who taught him
the book of pleasure
the book of plants
who nestled his specimens in barrels
like cradleboards
swaddled in layers —
leaves
earth

damp linen
silky moss
As he boarded ship for home
England, family, garden
Suckahanna vanished
quick knowing steps
so light upon the earth

iii
In 1629, John Parkinson —
Apothecary of London —
proposed for the delight of Queen Henrietta Marie
a garden
of all sort of pleasant flowers
which our English ayre will permit
to be noursed up —
"*Paradisi In Sole Paradisus Terrestris*" —
"an earthly paradise in the sun of paradise"

Parkinson invented Her name
elegant as calligraphy
Trachelium Americanum
Flore ruberrimo, siue Planta Cardinalis,
the rich crimson Cardinals flower
invocation of papal reds —
satin, velvet, serge

A century later, Linnaeus simplified
ordered
bestowed
the now familiar binomial
a nod to Flemish botanist, Matthias de L'Obel
Lobelia cardinalis
Cardinal Flower

iv
In Parkinson's earthly paradise
She was bedded with Bellflowers —
Canterbury
Coventry
Steeple
Hare

Faithful to Her wildish nature
She bloomed
coveted by admirers and acquisitors
planting Herself
in the imaginations of the Curious

v
All is noise
The air is of another life
and time
and place
In longing
She recalls voices

rising from different earth
from ground
where She is known
and reflected
citizen of streambank
bottomland
marsh
friend to hummingbird
swallowtail
bee

Beloved Daughter
of the Ones whose words
are bells
In Her water dreams they come
again and again
splashing
singing
praying

SHE AND *NANOKSHI*

> *...an intimate vocabulary that names each little part. To name and describe you must first see, and science polishes the gift of seeing...*
> Robin Wall Kimmerer

> *Puhpohwee... to swell up in stature suddenly and silently, from an unseen source of power...*
> Keewaydinoquay

i
For their laboratory work, Masters
and Johnson received death threats,
sent their children to safety.

Like botanists with field lens,
peering at stamens and pistils,
they fixed cameras on the genitals,

observing color changes, swellings,
exudations, recording what few have seen —
in the human female,

ninety seconds before orgasm,
the labia minora turn blood red.
Puhpohwee.

ii
Her flowers are velvety, tubular:
two scarlet lips, the upper
split into two long lobes, the lower

three-lobed, deeply cleft,
Her nectary hidden within.
As they mature, the petals turn

180 degrees, like the way
a baby, before birth, rotates
to the cephalic position.

iii
The story of The Flower and The Bird
reads like an erotic novel: She is rooted
in darkness. She summons *Nanokshi*

from the sky with Her red lips
Nanokshi hovers, wings beating
fifty times per second. Then

up and down, flower by perfect flower
Nanokshi sips Her nectar
wears Her pollen as a crown.

iv
If you can be still, *Nanokshi*
may look you in the eye, so close
you can hear wings humming,

resonance of bone and feather.
You can see the point of the long bill,
the red gorget's shimmer.

Nanokshi assesses your lips,
their redness, finds them
wanting, flies to the Beloved.

v
She and *Nanokshi* have grown together
out of the same place, shaped
to their own purpose. They are of

the soil. They are of the air. The sun
and moon are in them. They have made
each other, both of them, perfect.

MRS. SPOON AND MR. SMITH

> *Between my country — and the Others —*
> *There is a Sea —*
> *But Flowers — negotiate between us —*
> *As Ministry.*
> Emily Dickinson

i
Soon you will meet Mrs. Jim Spoon,
renowned Forest Potawatomi medicine woman,
but first a tale of Huron Smith,
author of six ethnobotanies.
In 1933 — his last afternoon —
he is at his desk,
before him a patchwork,
hundreds of specimens,
pressed and preserved.
In a twilight February hour —
driving family home —
all were killed by a train
of the Chicago, Milwaukee,
St. Paul & Pacific Railroad.

[I tell you this in another twilight February hour:
that train still runs not far from here —
a long whistle — Huron Smith at my shoulder.]

ii
In his paper on the Potawatomi,
Smith describes how an Indian agent
came every fall to "gather" —
Smith's word — children
for residential school, bemoans
their disinterest in their elders
sees loss,
but not theft
tragic parallel tracks:
preservation
destruction.

[It is said that when the agent came,
Keewaydinoquay hid under a waterfall.
The water masked her weeping.]

iii
Of Mr. Smith's Potawatomi informants,
Mrs. Spoon is said to be the most well-versed.
They traversed Wisconsin's near-boreal forests

harvesting winter stores. In a photo,
Mrs. Spoon beaded and beribboned.
Written under the photo, "*Emquatakwa.*"

iv
From Smith's field notes:
Joe Pye-Weed: *Fresh leaves are used
by the Potawatomi to make poultices for healing burns.
Mrs. Spoon used the root under the name, "maskwano'kuk"
(red top), as a medicine to clear up afterbirth*

Indian Pipe: '*According to Mrs. Spoon the proper name
of this is "mena'mabag weabsku'nakuk"
(white flower smells good) …used the roots
to make a tea for female troubles*

Common Evening Primrose: "*owesa'wanakuk*"
(*yellow top) …the tiny seeds are used for medicine,
but Mrs. Spoon did not say for what*

[*So many others!
So many plant friends!*]

v
Mrs. Spoon and Mr. Smith come to us
in fragments, like dreams recalled
upon awakening, ghosts in faded photos,

an obscure, century-old manuscript.
See them leaning together, heads
inclined, honored elder, esteemed

botanist, their most proximate sharing,
loving plants, spelling out the beautiful names,
syllable by precious syllable.

[*I do not find The Flower in Smith's Forest Potawatomi
report. Yet I imagine Her in conversation with Emquatakwa;
days of laughter, secrets, songs,
days of mourning and flames.*]

BAREFOOT

> "...not half so ragged as her heart,
> which is barefoot always — ."
> Emily Dickinson

> " — the rapture of losing my shoe in the Mud
> and going Home barefoot,
> wading for Cardinal Flowers..."
> Emily Dickinson

> "It was there that I found the poet Emily Dickinson. As I perched that large book between my skinned knees, alone in my need to be alone, her voice reached out from the pages and made friends with me..."
> Joy Harjo

i
Have you heard about the time
when Emily lost a shoe
in the mud, wading
for The Flower?

Tomboy Emily
who claimed rapture
barefoot heart

Barefoot Emily
much more moist
than virginal, white-laced, black bodice'd
Anthology Emily

Consider Emily's quatrain
White as an Indian Pipe
Red as a Cardinal Flower
Fabulous as a Moon at Noon
February Hour —

Sit with it for a while
Have a line tattooed on your thigh
Fabulous — the ancient form:
to speak, to say, to tell

Story-Teller Emily
who told Red

ii
At a plant sale — students
selling seedlings — I flush
to see *Tradescantia virginiana*

I want to say, do you know the tales
of the Tradescants, their exploits
and explorations, their curious — like flowers —

sex lives? Of course, I say not a word,
move on to the succulents, but I think
about John the Younger, far-seeing

Suckahanna, Huron Smith, *Emquatakwa*
living in my heart and mind. And Emily
absolutely for barefootedness

for reaching across time — poet
to poet, tomboy to tomboy
girl-child to girl-child.

iii
In Queen Henrietta's garden,
The Flower, you may recall, was planted
with the Bellflowers, a plant family

now known for having a female part
surrounded by five male parts —
clever cylinder for intricacies of fertilization

Her Scarlet expectations.

RED SHE IS

> *It is not your face in the lake I see —*
> *I find you nowhere that is here or there.*
> Jennifer Elise Foerster

> *Sacred red...is a condition inherent in certain*
> *beings who are of a certain order*
> *and possessed of a specific kind of power.*
> Paula Gunn Allen

i
The Flower appears in only one of Smith's
reports, described by *Kepeosatok*, Potawatomi
medicine man, living among the Meskwaki

Kepeosatok says that She can be ground
Her dust cast against storms
strewn on new graves

Kepeosatok says that when couples quarrel
She can be secretly mixed into meals
to prevent divorce, or added to old women's food

to, as one might say, pep things up
She is love medicine, love charm
Kepeosatok says this is women's business

The Flower is not named

ii
The Flower asks, why do you pore
over old papers when the sun shines
and robins splash in the birdbath?

Come outside!

iii
I kneel to the Names
the ones hidden, waiting, lost
the ones not mine to know

I ask permission to name The Flower
with a word from the Potawatomi — *Mskoze*
Said like this; mmm shkoh zeh
In my mouth *Mskoze* is silky moss
Mskoze translates as *Red She Is*
A verb

Red roots
Red grows
Red blooms

Red desires
Red ripens
Red bleeds

Red indwells the dreams of healers
oaks, poets, gardeners, the Curious
Red calls down the hummingbird

With gratitude, I ask The Flower to accept
this name and these poems as my offering

MSKOZE

> ...*from the dark we felt their soft*
> *presences at the edge of our mind*
> *and we heard their singing*
> Joy Harjo

> *Stories are alive,*
> *and they go where they wish.*
> Keewaydinoquay

All summer, every summer
Nanokshi and I wait
for Her season, for the hours

when the only sounds are clouds
in conversation. We wait
where She was planted

in the rain garden's still damp hollows
yet now She's made her own move
ablaze

on crumbling railroad ties —
nurse logs for wood fern
and willow herb

What I thought was a plant is a teacher
What I thought was my garden is not mine
is me

What I thought would be a simple word
is an unfolding, a sunrise
a door

How brilliant!
Her name abides in the dark beneath
healer singing in the forest

girl-child dipping toes in silt
In water and fire
She blooms

MIGWÉCH

> *This is memory shredded*
> *because it is impossible*
> *to hold with words even*
> *poetry.*
> *These memories were left here with the trees.*
> Joy Harjo

In the forests left alone
among the old trees
this word is spoken
migwéch

the sound of the forest
sparrow's high-pitched
melancholy
wind walking with leaves
river writing
on stones

the old ones know
if you press
against creases
and furrows
of a cottonwood
and whisper
migwéch
it would be enough

on a day like today
when sun lights
every leaf
every maple and oak
you could raise arms
in gratitude
cry *migwéch* for
the whole land
to hear

nado'wen —
the simplest sort
of healing —
would be its blessing
in return

PHOTO COURTESY OF GLENN ADELSON

An Onondaga elder once explained to me that
plants come to us when they are needed.
If we show them respect
by using them
and appreciating their gifts
they will grow stronger.
They will stay with us
as long as they are respected.
But if we forget about them, they will leave.

Robin Wall Kimmerer

MSKOZE / RED SHE IS

NOTES

Kathryn Dohrmann

EPIGRAPHS

When I don't know what to do, I go to the plants. To learn from the land, you need to be in the presence of a teacher.
Robin Wall Kimmerer

These words come from a 2023 interview with Robin Wall Kimmerer (European and Anishinaabe ancestry / Potawatomi woman of the Bear and Eagles clans) in the University of Wisconsin alumni magazine.
https://onwisconsin.uwalumni.com/the-teachings-of-plants/

On her webpage, Kimmerer describes herself as "mother, scientist, decorated professor, and enrolled member of the Citizen Potawatomi Nation." She is Distinguished Teaching Professor at the State University of New York College of Environmental Science and Forestry. Also the founding director of SUNY's Center for Native Peoples and the Environment, her research focuses on the role of ecological knowledge in habitat healing and restoration, as well as on the ecology of mosses. Kimmerer is widely known for her book, *Braiding Sweetgrass: Indigenous Wisdom, Scientific Knowledge, and the Teachings of Plants*. Her numerous awards include a MacArthur Foundation "genius grant" in 2022 and a National Humanities Medal in 2023.
https://www.robinwallkimmerer.com/about

INTRODUCTION

"A plant native to much of the Americas"

The Biota of North America Program (BONAP) is a useful source on the distribution of native plants. Information on *Lobelia cardinalis*, and other members of the genus, Lobelia, can be found here:
http://bonap.net/Napa/TaxonMaps/Genus/County/Lobelia

More general data on *Lobelia cardinalis*, as well as an image gallery, can be found at the Lady Bird Johnson Wildflower Center:
https://www.wildflower.org/gallery/species.php?id_plant=LOCA2

"the Potawatomi nations, for whom this place is home"

The decision to search for an Indigenous name in the Potawatomi language was not initially obvious to me. For thousands of years, a variety of Native peoples have inhabited and traveled through the southwestern Lake Michigan region. As John William Nelson writes in his book, *Muddy Ground: Native Peoples, Chicago's Portage, and the Transformation of a Continent*, this region (also known as the Chicago portage) has long been a vital—and sometimes contested—passageway from the Great Lakes to the Mississippi watershed.

The work of John Low, citizen of the Pokagon Band of Potawatomi, and historian at Ohio State, Newark, convinced me that Potawatomi was the language with which I should begin. In an article about land acknowledgements, Low says that there is "substantial confusion" (p. 20) about which Indigenous people can claim Chicago as a homeland. He asserts that Chicago is the ancestral home of the Potawatomi, and offers several arguments:

> a. in oral histories, no tribe other than the Potawatomi situates an origin story in Chicago;
>
> b. the existence of historic maps, representing the combined knowledge of tribal elders, archaeologists, and anthropologists, place the Potawatomi homeland along the southwestern shores of Lake Michigan;
>
> c. after the Beaver Wars (17th century battles fought over control of the fur trade in North America), during which Iroquois nations had driven Algonquian Indians (including the Potawatomi) westward, it was the Potawatomi who returned to their southwestern Lake Michigan homelands;
>
> d. at the 1933 Treaty of Chicago, only Potawatomi individuals signed and attended the negotiations. Signers of earlier treaties were predominantly Potawatomi as well;
>
> e. important chiefs in Chicago were Potawatomi, native settlements in the area had Potawatomi names (e.g. Waukegan), and, when non-natives inter-married indigenous individuals, they married into Potawatomi households;
>
> f. in a well-known 1917 U.S. Supreme Court case, it was the Pokagon Band of Potawatomi who sued to claim the Chicago lakefront, the only sovereign tribal nation to have ever done so. And it was that 1917 court case that the artist, Andrea Carlson (Ojibwe), used to justify her choice of the statement, "This is Potawatomi land," in a public art installation (and Land Acknowledgment) along the Chicago riverfront. https://native newsonline. net/arts-enter tainment/

native-in-the-arts-spotlight-visual-artist-andrea-carlson-talks-about-her-chicago-you-are-on-potawatomi-land-mural

Low continues: "*It was the Potawatomi who burned down Fort Dearborn—no one else was there. It was the Potawatomi from Indiana and Illinois who were walked out west on a Trail of Death—no one else has stories of removal from Chicago. Only the Potawatomi of northern Illinois and Indiana were forced onto reservations west of the Mississippi. Simon Pokagon (Pokagon Band Potawatomi) wrote in 1893 about Chicago as home at the 1893 World's Columbian Exposition in Chicago*" (p. 24).

Low concludes: "*If we objectively look at the evidence, the archives, and the available information, it is clear that Chicago is within the homelands of the Potawatomi. A Land Acknowledgment should not operate as a colonial erasure of that truth, and a proper Land Acknowledgment should promote the Potawatomi connections to this land so that it remains in the collective memory of all who care about Chicago.*" (p. 24).

https://johnlowpokagon.files.wordpress.com/2023/02/low-2022-3fall-win-chm-chicagohistory-vol46-no2.pdf

"*the very oldest trees in my neighborhood once heard the lush sounds of Potawatomi language.*"

My thinking about old trees having heard Potawatomi language began as a fanciful exercise. Then I read Rebecca Solnit's essay, "Day of the Dead," from her collection, *Orwell's Roses*. She writes: "*trees...felt as though they were the living witnesses of a past otherwise beyond our reach*" (p. 6). See more about this idea in the notes accompanying the last poem, particularly Solnit's term, "arboreal saeculum."

"*knowledge gathering*"

Joy Harjo, the 23rd United States poet laureate, and a member of the Muscogee (Creek) nation writes: "*My creative life, I have come to understand, finds energetics in traveling, either physically or through knowledge gathering...*" (p. 56). https://www.pw.org/content/the_field_of_stories_a_qa_with_joy_harjo

A Note on Naming...

In her introduction to the anthology, *When the Light of the World was Subdued, Our Light Came Through*, editor Joy Harjo addresses the complexities of using "American Indian" and "Native American." For the anthology, she elects to use these general terms: "Native," "Indigenous," or "Native Nations." These are the words I will use. When I cite or discuss particular individuals, I will try to honor the terminology they have chosen for themselves.

THE FLOWER

Epigraph

...plants are thought of as beings with their own histories, stories, beliefs, and way of life. Anishinaabe protocols require us to introduce plants just as we would introduce another human being.

Wendy Makoons Geniusz

Deconstructing the epigraph:

a. **The human beings**
   The epigraph was written by **Wendy Makoons Geniusz** (Cree and Métis), editor of *Plants Have So Much To Give Us, All We Have To Do Is Ask: Anishinaabe Botanical Teachings*, a book authored by her mother, Mary Siisip Geniusz (1948-2016). Wendy Makoons Geniusz is a Professor of Sociology at York University, where her work focuses on the decolonization and revitalization of Ojibwe language and culture. The words of the epigraph transport us into a lineage of Great Lakes Native medicine women and ethnobotanists.

   Mary Siisip Geniusz (Cree and Métis) spent much of her life in Wisconsin, learning from the Ojibwe tribe (which, she notes, is related linguistically and culturally to her Cree ancestors). She attributes the ideas in her book to Keewaydinoquay Peschel (1919-1999), an Anishinaabe/Ojibwe medicine woman (*Mashkikiiwikwe*) and ethnobotanist, to whom she was an apprentice and ceremonial/medicinal helper (*Oshkaabewis*).
   https://notablefolkloristsofcolor.org/portfolio/mary-siisip-geniusz/

   Keewaydinoquay Peschel (Anishinaabe/Ojibwe), was a prolific writer and dedicated teacher of the ethnobotany and world views of Great Lakes Indigenous people. In a collection of her materials housed at Harvard University, she is described as follows: *"Keewaydinoquay Pakawakuk Peschel (1919-1999) was an Anishinaabeg Elder of the Crane Clan. She was an ethnobotanist, teacher, medicine woman, and author."*
   https://hollisarchives.lib.harvard.edu/catalog/ecb00001_ecb00001c01476

   Keewaydinoquay was apprenticed at age nine for six years to **Nodjimahkwe** ("Healing Woman"), a venerated Anishinaabe healer. Keewaydinoquay, in her book, *Puhpowee for the People*, writes that Nodjimahkwe was *"heir to the traditional knowledge of the plant world among her people"* (p. *v*), and her *"knowledge of materia medica was truly astounding"* (p. *viii*). Mary Siisip Geniusz says that Nodjimahkwe could recite the names of her

teachers and their teachers in a chain going back four hundred years.
https://notablefolkloristsofcolor.org/portfolio/keewaydinoquay-pakawakuk- peschel/

b. The word, *Anishinaabe*

Anishinaabe is frequently encountered—in various spellings and usages—when exploring the Indigenous cultures of the Great Lakes Region. In the Ojibwe Word Glossary to *Plants Have So Much To Give Us, All We Have To Do Is Ask*, Wendy Makoons Geniusz defines *Anishinaabe* as an "*Indian, Chippewa or Ojibwe*" person (p. 334).

Geniusz explains that Keewaydinoquay used *Anishinaabe* to refer to "*... an Indian person of one of the Three Fires Nations: the Ojibwe or Chippewa, the Odaawa or Ottawa, the Boodewaadamii or Potawatomi*" (p. 334). She further notes that in storytelling, *Anishinaabe* is usually thought to mean "*Mankind*" (p. 334).

Wendy Makoons Geniusz, Mary Siisip Geniusz, and Keewaydinoquay work(ed) primarily within Ojibwe traditions. An on-line Ojibwe dictionary defines *Anishinaabe* as, "*(1) an Ojibwe, (2) an Indian (in contrast to a non-Indian), a Native (in contrast to a non-Native), and (3) a person, a human (in contrast to a non-human being).*"
https://ojibwe.lib.umn.edu/main-entry/anishinaabe-na

According to Robin Wall Kimmerer, the Potawatomi equivalent of Ojibwe's *Anishinaabe*, is *Neshnabé*. The Citizen Potawatomi Nation's on-line dictionary defines *Neshnabé* as "*1. An Indian 2. Original man and 3. Potawatomi.*"
http://potawatomidictionary.com/Dictionary/Word/5396.

Relatedly, the on-line dictionary of the Pokagon Band of Potawatomi defines *neshnabé* as a "native american person."
https://wiwkwebthegen.com/dictionary-word/neshnab%C3%A9
In these Notes, I try to use Neshnabé or Anishinaabe as my sources use them.

c. The concept of plants as persons

I first encountered these ideas in the chapter, "Relearning the Grammar of Animacy," in Kimmerer's *Braiding Sweetgrass*. As she began learning *Bodewadmimwen*, the language of her Potawatomi ancestors, Kimmerer encountered a way of thinking about "*a world of being, full of unseen energies that animate everything*" (p. 49).

For example, when Kimmerer discusses Keewaydinoquay's writings on fungi, we hear Keewaydinoquay Peschel's word for rising and emergence, *puhpohwee*: "*the force which causes mushrooms to push up from the earth overnight*" (p. 49). Keewaydinoquay (in *Puhpowee for the People*) says that *puhpohwee* means "*to swell up in stature suddenly and silently, from an unseen source of power*" (p. vii).

The grammar of animacy is beautiful and complex. A discussion of the word "it" can help us begin to understand. We recognize that there is a problem when we speak of another person as "it." For example, if someone were to say about an infant, "change its diapers," or "make it stop crying," we would see a problem in the relationship between the speaker and the infant. The use of "it" would make us uncomfortable. There is an implied disrespect, and a lack of kinship. We might worry about the infant's safety.

Kimmerer explains that Indigenous languages use a language of animacy to speak about — and to speak to — our larger family: the nonhuman (or more-than-human) living world. This is a family of plants, water, fire, mountains, and places. In an interview, Kimmerer says: "*in Potawatomi, the case we have is animate, and it is impossible to speak of other beings as 'it.'*" Thus, a tree is not an "it." A lake is not an "it." A plant is not an "it." In her writing and speaking, Kimmerer asserts a "*personhood of all beings.*" To recognize plant personhood is to offer respect and restore relationship.
https://onbeing.org/programs/robin-wall-kimmerer-the-intelligence-of- plants-2022/

Other Indigenous writers also employ the language of animacy. For example, Paula Gunn Allen (1939-2008, Laguna Pueblo and Sioux), in the Introduction to her 1986 book, *The Sacred Hoop: Recovering the Feminine in American Indian Traditions*, writes: "*When I was small, my mother told me that animals, insects, and plants are to be treated with the kind of respect one customarily affords to high-status adults.* "*Life is a circle, and everything has its place in it,*' *she would say. That's how I met the sacred hoop...*" (p. 1).

AIR FROM ANOTHER LIFE AND TIME AND PLACE

Title

The words of the title are borrowed from Seamus Heaney's poem, "A Kite for Aibhín" (in his collection, *Human Chain*). In turn, Heaney borrowed these words from a poem called "L'Aquilone" by Giovanni Pascoli (1855 – 1912) — a work that Heaney translated.

The first epigraph

...the strange blooms they loved so much set seed in the rich dark mulch of human desires...
Jennifer Potter

In an extensively researched book, *Strange Blooms: The Curious Adventures of the John Tradescants*, Jennifer Potter explores the lives of British plant collector, John Tradescant and his son, John the Younger, during the time when Europe transitioned from "superstition and wonder to the dawning of science" (p. xxiii). (See more about the Tradescants in *Part ii*, below.)

The second epigraph

...And sometimes in our water dreams, we pitiful land-dwellers in longing recall, and singing make spirits ready to follow; bakobii* (*Go down into the water.) Kimberly M. Blaeser

Kimberly M. Blaeser is Anishinaabe from the White River Reservation, a professor at the University of Wisconsin-Milwaukee, a faculty member in the MFA program at the Institute of American Indian Arts, and a Wisconsin Poet Laureate (2015 – 2016). The epigraph is from the poem, "Dreams of Water Bodies," first published in her poetry collection, *Copper Yearning*, and anthologized in Joy Harjo's edited collection, *When the Light of the World was Subdued, Our Songs Came Through: A Norton Anthology of Native Nations Poetry*.

Part i

The concept of the Mistaken Zygote is borrowed from *Women Who Run with the Wolves*, the classic feminist reinterpretation of European folk tales by Jungian psychoanalyst, Clarissa Pinkola Estes. The Mistaken Zygote is a child (often, though not always, a girl) who — using a stork metaphor — is "dropped" at the wrong house. She is raised in a family where she is too *something*: too difficult, too sensitive, too curious, too wild, too angry, too sexual — *too much*. In Hans Christian Anderson's, "The Ugly Duckling," the Mistaken Zygote is akin to the swan raised with ducklings: someone perpetually out of place. In Clarissa Pinkola Estes' Jungian retelling, the child's journey to the right place, the home ground, is unconscious — until, thankfully, it isn't.

Part ii

Although in this poem we only meet John the Younger, both father and son—the John Tradescants — were gardeners to royalty and nobility, and collectors of plants and rarities. If you went to London during the 17th century, it was imperative to visit "Tradeskins Ark," which became the founding collection of the Ashmolean Museum at Oxford.

Although there were other well-known plant collectors at the time in England and on the Continent, the Tradescants live on in memory. As noted above, Jennifer Potter examines the survival and growth of their reputations in *Strange Blooms; The Curious Adventures of the John Tradescants*.

The lives of the Tradescants have also been captured in historical fiction, notably in a two-volume series by Phillippa Gregory: *Earthly Joys* and *Virgin Earth*. These novels, with their vividly imagined personalities and emotions enliven the Tradescants. In Gregory's erotic storytelling, *Suckahanna* is created as the Powhatan "wife" of John the Younger. Like the plant in these poems, *Suckahanna* is at one with water.

The Powhatan word, "*suckahanna*," has also intrigued other artists; for example, a public art installation in Virginia by Jann Rosen-Queralt is titled, "Cultivus Loci: Suckahanna."

https://www.americansforthearts.org/by-program/networks-and-councils/public-art-network/public-art-year-in-review-database/cultivus-loci-suckahanna

Part iii

The garden proposed by John Parkinson (1567-1650), The Apothecary of London, was designed for Queen Henrietta Marie, the French Catholic bride of King Charles I. A detailed description of this garden is available in Project Gutenberg's eBook version of *Paradisi In Sole Paradisus Terrestris*.

Parkinson notes that the "*rich crimson Cardinals flower*" is "*...commendable only for the great bush of so orient red crimson flowers*" ... and that it "*growth neere the riuer of Canada, where the French plantation in America is seated*."
https://www.gutenberg.org/files/69425/69425-h/69425-h.htm#Page_356

Part iv

"Curious" derives from the Latin, *curioso*, meaning full of care or consideration. Many of the varied uses of this word have become obsolete; we tend to think of it now either in the sense of inquisitiveness, or as something that is surprising or strange.

However, Jennifer Potter (in *Strange Blooms*) notes that in the 1600s, to be called "curious," was a "mark of distinction," both intellectually and socially (pp. xiv). It reflected an interest in the modern world, in art and science, and it had a particular meaning when applied to gardening. To be a "curious gardener," meant you belonged to a special group of individuals who collected and grew rare plants, and who exchanged information and plant material with other collectors and growers. For Potter, a curious gardener was both a "state of mind and an aspiration" (p. xxiv).

Part v

The line "again and again" reflects an explanation offered by Keewaydinoquay. She explains that plants used for sacred materials (e.g. smoking materials in ceremonial pipes) are "talked over" from their first buds in spring to the point at which they are harvested. On page 26 of *Gift of Bear*, Keewaydinoquay writes: "*These chosen plants will have known from the very beginning of their vernal efforts that their products of that season are marked for spiritual purposes. (Of course no plants are ever decimated: part of the promise to them, as to all harvested vegetation, is that they shall be well-treated—that their grandchildren shall live after them...*").

SHE AND NANOKSHI

Title

Nanokshi is the Potawatomi word for hummingbird, used for both males and females. See the Citizen Potawatomi dictionary for pronunciation. https://www.potawatomidictionary.com/Dictionary/Word/5064

Epigraph 1

...an intimate vocabulary that names each little part. To name and describe you must first see, and science polishes the gift of seeing...
Robin Wall Kimmerer

As a person trained in scientific botany, Kimmerer writes in *Braiding Sweetgrass*, "*I honor the strength of the language that has become a second tongue to me*" (pp. 48–49). From that statement, though, she moves to a critique: "*...something is missing...the same something that swells around you and in you when you listen to the world. Science can be a language of distance which reduces a being to its working parts: it is a language of objects. The language scientists speak, however precise, is based upon a profound error in grammar, an omission, a grave loss in translation from the native languages of these shores...In the three syllables of this new word [Puhpohwee]...I could see an entire process of close observation in the damp morning woods, the formulation of a theory for which English has no equivalent. The makers of this word understood a world of being, full of unseen energies that animate everything. I've cherished it for many years, as a talisman...The language that holds Puhpohwee, is one that I wanted to speak...when I learned that the word for rising, for emergence, belonged to the language of my ancestors, it became a signpost for me.*"

Kimmerer continues: "*In fact, I learned that the mystical word, "Puhpohwee," is used not only for mushrooms, but also for certain other shafts that rise mysteriously in the night*" (p.54).

Epigraph 2

Puhpohwee... "to swell up in stature suddenly and silently, from an unseen source of power."

Keewaydinoquay Peschel

Keewaydinoquay's definition of "Puhpowee" (p. 48) is explored in her book, *Puhpowee for the People*.

Part i

William Masters and Virginia Johnson began their collaboration in 1957 at the Department of Obstetrics and Gynecology at Washington University in St. Louis. They founded the Reproductive Biology Research Foundation (later re-named the Masters and Johnson Institute), where they worked from 1978 – 1994.

Exudations, swellings, and color changes during sexual arousal reflect the impact of blood flow to the genitals. These occur regardless of biological sex, due to the shared embryonic structures of the urogenital system.

Part ii

The Ruby-throated Hummingbird, *Archilochus colubris*, is the primary breeding hummingbird of eastern North America. https://www.allaboutbirds.org/guide/Ruby-throated_Hummingbird

In the line, "flower by perfect flower," the word *perfect* is employed as botanists use it: to describe individual flowers that have both male and female organs. *Lobelia cardinalis* (here, "The Flower") is not only perfect, but also *protandrous* — the male flower structures mature first, producing pollen. A few days later, in the female phase, a white stigma matures and become receptive to pollen. The stigma is a female part of the flower — a sticky bulb in the center where the pollen lands and starts the fertilization process. The pollen travels from flower to flower on the hummingbird's head. You can see the white stigma on the image left.

Photo: https://www.usgs.gov/media/images/lobelia-cardinalis-3-cardinal-flower-howard-county-md

Part iii

The ideas in this section are influenced by the writings of Susan Griffin, particularly the poetic essay, "Forests," in *Woman and Nature: The Roaring Inside Her*, a singular work of ecofeminist thinking.

MRS SPOON AND MR SMITH

Epigraph

> *Between my country—and the Others—*
> *There is a Sea—*
> *But Flowers—negotiate between us—*
> *As Ministry.*

Emily Dickinson

An image of this poem, in Dickinson's handwriting, can be found at this link: https://www.edickinson.org/editions/1/image_sets/12175971

Part i

Huron H. Smith (1883-1933)

An image of Huron Smith gazing at a desk filled with preserved plant specimens can be found on the Milwaukee Public Museum website: https://artsandculture.google.com/story/GgWBpBucHdv4Jg?hl=en

In 1917, Huron Smith left Chicago's Field Museum of Natural History to lead the Botany Department at the Milwaukee Public Museum. During the 1920s and into the early 1930s, he systematically collected the plant usage knowledge of six Wisconsin Indian tribes. This occurred during an era when the knowledge of elders generally was not being transmitted to younger tribal members. His manuscripts on the Forest Potawatomi and other Wisconsin Indians can be found on-line in the ethnobotany section of the Milwaukee Public Museum:
https://archive.mpm.edu/research-collections/botany/online-collections-research/ethnobotany

Smith died in an auto-train collision in 1933. A hauntingly titled ("TRAIN BLOTS OUT FAMILY") *New York Times* obituary gives Smith's death date (February 25), the time (shortly before 7 pm), and even the engineer's name ("Fred Urtibe...at the throttle"). The accident occurred on Waukegan Road in Glenview, Illinois, a few miles from my home. https://timesmachine.nytimes.com/timesmachine/1933/02/26/99907928.html?pageNumber=74

The *In Memoriam* section of Smith's Potawatomi manuscript (posthumously published later that year) notes that the Forest Potawatomi work was already in page proof, and that on the day of his death, Smith had been working on the Winnebago [Ho-Chunk/Hocąk] manuscript: "*...the last day of his life had been devoted to his Winnebago paper and he had carried on this work up to within about three hours prior to his death, leaving the notes and data in place upon his desk where they could be taken up immediately upon his return.*"

https://archive.mpm.edu/sites/default/files/downloads/ethnobotany/potawatomi/publication.pdf

Part ii

Huron Smith describes the "gathering" of Forest Potawatomi children as follows: *"Children of school age are gathered together in the fall and taken to the various Indian schools, most of them going to-the Lac du Flambeau Ojibwe school, while some go away as far as Flandreau, South Dakota. Those of high school age go to Haskell University"* (p.23). https://archive.mpm.edu/sites/default/files/downloads/ethnobotany/potawatomi/publication.pdf Haskell University is now Haskell Indian Nations University (Lawrence, Kansas). https://haskell.edu/.

For the ideas represented in these lines, *"tragic parallel tracks/preservation/destruction,"* I am indebted to Wendy Makoons Geniusz (Cree and Métis heritage, raised with Ojibwe language and culture), especially her 2015 book, *Our Knowledge is Not Primitive: Decolonizing Botanical Anishinaabe Teachings*. The juxtaposition of early ethnobotanical scholarship as simultaneously preservative and destructive is hers, as are cautions about the ways in which non-Native scholars portray Native life and concepts.

Speaking as a scholar in American Indian studies, Makoons writes: "...*colonialism is about one people completely taking over another people. It is not just about land. It does not end when one government gains control of another. It is about one society absorbing another society, and it continues until that process is accomplished. Yes, lands and governments are taken over, but so is every other facet of life, including language, culture, religion, knowledge, bodies, and beings. ...For Indigenous people, colonization was not just economic and physical exploitation. It was also the exploitation and subjugation of our knowledge, our minds, and our very beings"* (p. 2).

She continues: *"One multifaceted mechanism, which continues to maintain this power structure, is the colonization of knowledge. Those charged with carrying out various assimilation tactics were taught to view native knowledge as "primitive" or "evil," and as a result they often prevented its continued dispersal within native communities. Native people were also taught to view their knowledge as "wrong" or "inferior" and non-native knowledge as "right" or "superior," and having such views many naturally chose what was made to look like the better knowledge"* (p. 3).

Makoons asserts that botanic colonization was both destructive and preservative. Once Indigenous knowledge was viewed as inferior, the holder of that knowledge might share it—or part with it—for a price indicative of its perceived, low value. Others, seeing the consequences of assimilation, would entrust their knowledge to researchers, hoping that at least some of it would be preserved.

For further discussion of this topic, see Lucille Brockway's *Science and Colonial Expansion: The Role of the British Royal Botanic Gardens*. Brockway explores "economic botany," a process whereby British botanists appropriated and profited from the plant knowledge of Indian healers in the New World.

Part iii

Smith worked with the Forest Potawatomi in September of 1925 and June of 1926, primarily near Laona, Wisconsin. He writes that *"The Potawatomi have several medicine men and women who guard their secrets very jealously"* (p. 29).

Smith described Mrs. Jim Spoon (*Emquatakwa*) as his most knowledgeable informant: *"a medicine woman of more than local repute and the writer accompanied her when she procured her winter store of medicinal plants. She was by far the best versed of any of the informants and often traveled great distances to get the plants she desired"* (p. 12). https://archive.mpm.edu/sites/default/files/downloads/ethno-botany/potawatomi/publication.pdf

Plate 3, Figure 1 of the Potawatomi report is a photo of Mrs. Spoon (*Emquatakwa*). It is captioned: *"Mrs. Jim Spoon, Laona, Wisc., famous medicine woman."* (Neg. No. 48640) https://archive.mpm.edu/sites/default/files/downloads/ethnobotany/potawatomi/photos.pdf

> Mrs. Amquon, wife of Jim Spoon, assistant chief and medicine man of the Pottawattomie Indian tribe, was seen on our streets Friday. She was beautifully decorated in bright ribbons, beads and other ornaments to suit her royal majesty and was headed toward the photo gallery.

More photos of Mrs. Spoon (*Emquatakwa*) can be found in the Appendix to Smith's Potawatomi report. On July 6, 1899, well before she worked with Huron Smith, *Emquatakwa* (here called "Mrs. Amquon") was described on page 8 of the *Wood County Reporter* (Grand Rapids, Wisconsin). https://www.newspapers.com/article/wood-county-reporter-1899-potawatomi-mrs/66945245/

Part iv

An example of plant usage knowledge and the syllable-by-syllable approach to Forest Potawatomi plant names can be found here. This is *Acer rubrum*, Red Maple:

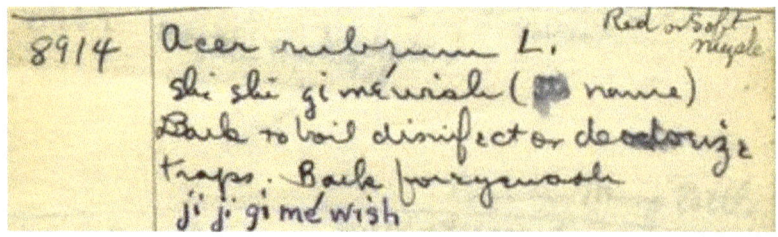

Huron Smith notes that a Forest Potawatomi tribal member, Joe Ellick, had created a Potawatomi syllabary (327 syllables), used for writing to relatives, about 55 years prior to his report (likely in the early 1880s). https://archive.mpm.edu/research-collections/botany/collections/ethnobotany/tribe-photos/potawatomi

The need for communication with far-flung family members can be understood better by reading Huron Smith's discussion of Forest Potawatomi history: "...*Potawatomi bands are spread over a wide area. Between 1789 and 1867 through 43 treaties, the Potawatomi were forced to cede their lands between Wisconsin and Ohio. Most Potawatomi were forcibly removed west but some remained in their ceded territory and were referred to as "strolling Potawatomis." Some of the "strolling" Potawatomis who remained in Milwaukee and Waukesha counties migrated to Forest County, Wis. to avoid forced removal west...*" https://artsandculture.google.com/story/GgWBpBucHdv4Jg?hl=en

BAREFOOT

Epigraph 1

> "...*not half so ragged as her heart, which is barefoot always—.*"
>
> Emily Dickinson

Emily Dickinson (1830-1886) wrote the phrase, "*her heart which is barefoot always,*" in a letter to Elizabeth Chapin Holland (1823-1896), whose husband, Josiah Gilbert Holland, was an editor at the Springfield Republican newspaper. In her many letters to Holland, Dickinson shared news of her garden, household happenings, current reading, and family health. Holland and Dickinson also exchanged plants. The full quote is found in a February, 1885 letter from Dickinson to Holland: "*Tell Katrina about the Buttercups that Emily tills, and the Butterflies Emily chases, not catches, alas, because her Hat is torn — but not half so ragged as her Heart, which is barefoot always—*" http://archive.emilydickinson.org/correspondence/holland/l966.html

See also R.B. Sewall's *The Life of Emily Dickinson, Vol. II*, pp. 593-625.

Epigraph 2

> "*—the rapture of losing my shoe in the Mud and going Home barefoot, wading for Cardinal Flowers...*"
>
> Emily Dickinson

In 1882, Emily linked her mother with *Lobelia cardinalis* in what Judith Farr, in the *Gardens of Emily Dickinson*, calls a "sorrowful reminiscence of her childhood" (pp. 52-53).

> "*Two things I have lost with Childhood – the rapture of losing my shoe in the Mud and going Home barefoot, wading for Cardinal flowers and the mothers reproof which was more for my sake than her weary own for she frowned with a smile [—] now Mother and Cardinal flower are parts of a closed world—.*"

See also R.B. Sewall's, *The Life of Emily Dickinson, Vol. 1*, p. 88.

Epigraph 3

> "*It was there that I found the poet Emily Dickinson. As I perched that large book between my skinned knees, alone in my need to be alone, her voice reached out from the pages and made friends with me...*"
>
> Joy Harjo

In an unflinchingly honest memoir, *Poet Warrior*, Joy Harjo describes finding refuge in words during her chaotic childhood. In second grade, when she was given a poetry book on her birthday, she encountered Emily Dickinson for the first time. She recognized their kinship, their mutual aloneness, and their need to be alone. Citing Dickinson's poem, "I'm nobody! Who are you?" she recalls the realization that Dickinson was a friend—across time and culture—who also found refuge in words (p. 37). She writes: "*...It was the same year [second grade] that I asked for books of poetry for my birthday. I was given Louis Untermeyer's Golden Treasure of Poetry. It was there that I found the poet Emily Dickinson. As I perched that large book between my skinned knees, alone in my need to be alone, her voice reached out from the pages and made friends with me. I could hear her, though we were years, miles, landscapes, and cultures away from each other*" (p. 37).

In Part I of her memoir, in a chapter titled "Ancestral Roots," Harjo composes a poem for her young self, "Girl-Warrior," who "*spoke freely with the earth/And the plants, the animals/That roamed in the yard of the small house/Where her family lived/She was most herself when she was alone/And could hear the thrumming curiosity/Of the Creator who was pleased/With creation/* (p. 31).

There was more than aloneness that she shared with Dickinson (though as an eight-year-old she might not have known it), and that was a deep immersion in the natural world. Her memoir poetically continues: "*Baby brown-skinned girl/Patted out mud circles/And fed them to her friends/The frogs, the horny toads/the roly-poly bugs/Even the bees who would alight/Before they flew off to find sweetness/To make more sweetness* (p. 31). She also tells a story of being watched by an elder robin, and how he and his colleagues decided that she was a hybrid — half human/half bird (p. 62). Her memoir is full of otherworldly encounters with owls and robins and pine trees.

Part i

"My barefoot rank is better"

On June 7, 1862, in a letter to Thomas Wentworth Higginson, Dickinson wrote the phrase, *"my barefoot rank is better."* Higginson (1823–1911) was a Unitarian minister, author, politician, and abolitionist. In an April 1862 article in the Atlantic Monthly, "Letter to a Young Contributor," he encouraged and advised young writers. In response, Dickinson, then thirty-one, sent him a letter and four poems, the beginning of a correspondence — and sharing of poems—that lasted until her death. https://www.emilydickinsonmuseum.org/thomas-wentworth-higginson-1823-1911-correspondent/

In one of these letters, Higginson suggested that Dickinson's work was not ready for publication. In reply, she assured him that publication was not her intent: *"I smile when you suggest that I delay "to publish"— that being foreign to my thought, as Firmament to Fin — If fame belonged to me, I could not escape her — if she did not, the longest day would pass me on the chase-and the approbation of my Dog, would forsake me-then-My Barefoot-Rank is better—* https://archive.emilydickinson.org/correspondence/higginson/l265.html

Dickinson wrote this quatrain in a letter to Mabel Todd Loomis in the early 1870s:

White as an Indian Pipe
Red as a Cardinal Flower
Fabulous as a Moon at Noon
February Hour —

(The poem is listed as Fr 1193 in the R.E. Franklin edition of Dickinson's poems.)

In *The Gardens of Emily Dickinson*, Judith Farr speculates about the meaning of this poem, asking, for example, if *"fires in February blaze with a cardinal flower's scarlet?"* (p. 271). Farr asserts that, for Emily Dickinson, *"Expectations were always scarlet."* (p. 271).

RED SHE IS

Epigraph 1

> *It is not your face in the lake I see—*
> *I find you nowhere that is here or there.*
>
> Jennifer Elise Foerster

Jennifer Elise Foerster is a poet and teacher, author of three poetry collections, and Associate Editor for Joy Harjo's anthology, *When the Light of the World Was Subdued Our Songs Came Through: A Norton Anthology of Native Nations Poetry*. She is a member of the Muscogee (Creek) Nation of Oklahoma and lives in San Francisco. The epigraph is from a poem titled, "My silhouette, fossil of the drowned town's scroll," published in her collection, *The Maybe Bird*.

Epigraph 2

> Sacred red...is
> a condition inherent in
> certain beings who are
> of a certain order
> and possessed of a specific kind of power.
>
> Paula Gunn Allen

Full quote:

"The symbolism contained in tribal ceremonial literature is not symbolic in the Western literary or psychoanalytic sense; "corn" is not shorthand for dinner; "lake" does not allude to economic prosperity via fishing industries; "red" as used by the Lakota in reference to ceremonialism doesn't stand for "sacred" or "earth," but is the quality of a being the color of whom when perceived in a sacred manner is red. Red in this context is a psychic rather than a physical condition. Sacred red is not a consequence of light refraction and excitation of special oracular cells. It is a condition inherent in certain beings who are of a certain order and possessed of a specific kind of power" (p. 23 in Paula Gunn Allen's, *Grandmothers of the Light; A Medicine Woman's Sourcebook*).

Part iii

At the time of his interviews in the 1920s with Huron Smith, *Kepeosatok* (John McIntosh), was eighty-three years of age. He was known across several states as "renowned medicine man." *Kepeosatok* was born Prairie Potawatomi, but married into and lived with the Meskawki community. He loaned Huron Smith his notebooks (with formulas written in Meskawki language), and provided extensive plant information, as well as Indigenous plant names. Other Meskawki informants also added Indigenous plant names. https://archive.mpm.edu/sites/default/files/downloads/ethnobotany/meskwaki/publication.pdf

MSKOZE

Epigraph 1

The epigraph is excerpted from Joy Harjo's poem, "Exile of Memory": *"We could not see our ancestors as we climbed up/ To the edge of destruction/ But from the dark we felt their soft presences at the edge of our mind/ And we heard them singing"* (*An American Sunrise*, p. 16).

Epigraph 2

Mary Siisip Geniusz writes that stories and teaching spirits are far older than humans, and that they are aware, autonomous, and "cognizant" beings. She attributes the phrase, "Stories are alive and they go where they wish," to Keewaydinoquay. https://notablefolkloristsofcolor.org/portfolio/mary-siisip-geniusz/#:~:text=Story%20was%20a%20frequent%20topic,storytellers%20working%20with%20the%20Aadizookaanag

In the Citizen Potawatomi Nation's Dictionary, *Mskoze* is defined as "red he/she is," and it is tagged as a describing verb. https://www.potawatomidictionary.com/Dictionary/Word/4597. Justin Neely, the director of the Citizen Potawatomi Nation's language department, writes that Potawatomi is primarily a language of verbs. This is the case with words that we might usually think of as nouns or adjectives in English. For Neely's discussion of red as a verb, see this brief essay. https://www.potawatomi.org/blog/2020/08/28/language-update-august-2020/

Neely's longer explication of "red" in conversational Potawatomi, can be found here: https://theswissbay.ch/pdf/Books/Linguistics/Mega%20linguistics%20pack/North%20American/Algic/Potawatomi%2C%20Conversational%20%28Neely%29.pdf.

MIGWÉCH

> *This is memory shredded because it is impossible*
> *to hold with words even poetry.*
> *These memories were left here with the trees.*
>
> Joy Harjo

Epigraph

The epigraph is taken from Joy Harjo's poem, "How to Write a Poem in Time of War" (*Weaving Sundown in a Scarlet Light*, pp. 71–74).

In her essay, "Days of the Dead," pages 3–14 in *Orwell's Roses*, Rebecca Solnit introduces the term, "arboreal saeculum." She explains that a saeculum is "the span of time in which something is in living memory," and she offers the following examples: the last person who saw the last passenger pigeon, or the last survivor of the bombing of Hiroshima, or the last surviving prisoner of a Nazi concentration camp.

The old trees with whom I live have been witnesses to an age, to their own saeculum, in which many of the people passing under their canopies were speaking Potawatomi.

The Potawatomi words, *Migwéch* and *Nado'wen*, can be found in Potawatomi on-line dictionaries. *Migwéch* means "thank you."

https://www.potawatomidictionary.com/Dictionary/Word/4000

Nado'wen is defined as "healing" in the Citizen Potawatomi Nation Dictionary https://www.potawatomidictionary.com/Dictionary/Word/4941, and as the "act of healing" in the Pokagon Band of Potawatomi Dictionary. https://wiwkweb-thegen.com/dictionary-word/nadowen

CLOSING EPIGRAPH

> *An Onondaga elder once explained to me that*
> *plants come to us when they are needed.*
> *If we show them respect*
> *by using them*
> *and appreciating their gifts*
> *they will grow stronger.*
> *They will stay with us*
> *as long as they are respected.*
> *But if we forget about them, they will leave.*
>
> Robin Wall Kimmerer

The epigraph is part of a story that Robin Wall Kimmerer tells near the end of *Gathering Moss: A Natural and Cultural History of Mosses* (p. 161). The story concerns plants and knowledge, timing and gifts.

BIBLIOGRAPHY

Allen, P.G. (1991). *Grandmothers of the light: A medicine woman's sourcebook.* Beacon Press.

Allen, P. G. (1986). *The sacred hoop: Recovering the feminine in American Indian traditions.* Beacon Press.

Blaeser, K. (2019). *Copper yearning.* Holy Cow Press.

Brockway, L. (2002). *Science and colonial expansion: The role of the British Royal Botanic Gardens.* Yale University Press.

Estes, C. P. (1992). *Women who run with the wolves.* Ballantine Books.

Farr, J. (2004). *The gardens of Emily Dickinson.* Harvard University Press.

Foerster, J.E. (2022). *The maybe bird.* The Song Cave.

Franklin, R.W. (Ed.). (2005). *The complete poems of Emily Dickinson (Reading Edition).* Belknap Press.

Geniusz, M. S. (2015). *Plants have so much to give us, all we have to do is ask: Anishinaabe botanical teachings.* University of Minnesota Press.

Geniusz, W. M. (2009). *Our knowledge is not primitive: Decolonizing botanical Anishinaabe teachings.* Syracuse University Press.

Gregory, P. (2005). *Earthly joys.* Washington Square Press.

Gregory, P. (2006). *Virgin earth.* Atria Books.

Griffin, S. (1978). *Women and nature: The roaring inside her.* Harper & Row.

Harjo, J. (2023). *Weaving sundown in a scarlet light.* W.W. Norton and Company.

Harjo, J. (2021). *Poet warrior.* W.W. Norton and Company.

Harjo, J. (Ed.). (2020). *When the light of the world was subdued, our light came through.* W.W. Norton.

Harjo, J. (2019). *An American sunrise.* W.W. Norton and Company.

Heaney, S. (2011). *Human chain*. Farrar, Straus and Giroux.

Kimmerer, R.W. (2013). *Braiding sweetgrass: Indigenous wisdom, scientific knowledge, and the teachings of plants*. Milkweed Editions.

Kimmerer, R.W. (2003). *Gathering moss: A natural and cultural history of mosses*. Oregon State University.

Nelson, J.W. (2023). *Muddy ground: Native peoples, Chicago's portage, and the transformation of a continent*. University of North Carolina Press.

Peschel, K. (1998). *Puhpohwee for the people: A narrative account of some uses of fungi among the Ahnishinaubeg*. Botanical Museum of Harvard History, Cambridge, MA.

Peschel, K. (1977). *KinnicKinnick "Gift of Bear" (an origin tale never before recorded, how to use bearberry for teas, emergency food, treating diabetes and internal infections) (Mukwah Miskomin)*. Miniss Kitigan Drum, Garden Island, Michigan (7th printing).

Potter, J. (2006). *Strange blooms: The curious adventures of the John Tradescants*. London, Atlantic Books.

Sewall, R. B. (1974). *The life of Emily Dickinson, Vols. I and II*. Farrar, Straus and Giroux.

Solnit, R. (2021). *Orwell's roses*. Viking Press.

GRATITUDE —

To my supportive fellow writers and teachers: Lois Baer Barr, Cynthia T. Hahn, the late Karin Bente Gordon, Benjamin Goluboff, Timothy Muskat

To Glenn Adelson, for being a generous plant guide

To the Milwaukee Public Museum, for maintaining an invaluable collection of Indigenous ethnobotany

To the Indigenous women whose poems and writings have influenced my poetry and relationship with the natural world

To Angel Ackerman and Gayle F. Hendricks at Parisian Phoenix for their many talents and steadfast support

ABOUT THE AUTHOR

Kathryn Dohrmann has taught for many years in both the Psychology and Environmental Studies Departments at Lake Forest College. Her poems have been published in *CALYX: A Journal of Art and Literature for Women, The Chicago Tribune, The A-3 Review, The Ekphrastic Review, The Last Stanza Poetry Journal, OPEN: Journal of Arts and Letters,* and others. A finalist in the Gwendolyn Brooks Open Mic and WBEZ poet laureate competitions, she was also a participant in the Poetic Dialogue Project; her poems from that project—The Pandora Memos—have been anthologized in *Collaborative Vision* and *All About Eve*. Her chapbook, *Archaeomythology* (the first volume of the Stark Ravine Mad Series), was published in 2025 by Parisian Phoenix Publishing.

www.ingramcontent.com/pod-product-compliance
Lightning Source LLC
LaVergne TN
LVHW050138080526
838202LV00061B/6523